LEARNING CURVE

GARY BECK

This publication is a creative work protected in full by all applicable copyright laws, as well as by misappropriation, trade secret, unfair competition, and other applicable laws. No part of this book may be reproduced or transmitted in any manner without written permission from Winter Goose Publishing, except in the case of brief quotations embodied in critical articles or reviews. All rights reserved.

Winter Goose Publishing
45 Lafayette Road #114
North Hampton, NH 03862

www.wintergoosepublishing.com
Contact Information: info@wintergoosepublishing.com

Learning Curve

COPYRIGHT © 2021 by Gary Beck

First Edition, February 2021

Cover Design & Formatting by Winter Goose Publishing

ISBN: 978-1-952909-06-1

Published in the United States of America

*To Nancy, companion through thick and thin,
who keeps learning.
Love, Gary*

CONTENTS

Dancing in the Wind 1
Travelogue 2
Fundamentally 3
Enemies 4
Seasonal Awakening 7
Accidents Will Happen 8
Ecce Homo 9
Temperate Zone 11
Separate, but… 12
Homeless 13
Holiday 14
Blue Jays 15
Manhattan Landlord 16
Limits 18
Homeless II 20
Holiday II 21
Blue Jays II 22
Digital Control 23
Neighborhoods 24
Homeless III 25
Holiday III 26
Blue Jays III 27
Matriculation 28

Diminishing Garments	30
Park Flow	31
Comparative Assessment	32
Homeless IV	34
Holiday IV	35
Blue Jays IV	36
Weathervane	39
Unequal Crisis	40
Homeless V	41
Turmoil	42
Possessed	45
Vista	46
Caught	48
Information Gap	49
Deceptive Words	50
Homeless VI	52
Emergency Aid	53
Fib, or …	54
Proportionate Response	55
Unvalued Relics	56
Cityscape	58
Advanced Forecast	59
Gunfire Serenade	60
Homeless VII	61
Park Entertainment	62

National News 63
Urban Reaches 64
Allotment 65
Righteous Speech 66
Homeless VIII 69
Celestial Reckonings 70
Camera Serenade 71
Fading Pleasure 72
Pity the Children 73
Clamor 74
Trauma Time 75
Conflict 76
Rotations 77
Short Duration 79
Record Keeping 80
Abundant Tears 81
Summer Parkscape 82
Business as Usual 83
Degrees 84
Accused 85
Lesser Choices 86
Patterns of Deception 87
Common Practice 88
The More Deceived 89
Urban Polluters 90

Candidate	91
Damming the Electronic Stream	92
Welcome Mat	93
Onslaught	94
Pressure Points	95
Summer Pace	96
Medical Visit	97
Summertime	98
Civilization	99
Stadiums	100
Excuses	101
Declarations	102
Acknowledgements	103

Dancing in the Wind

The tree sways gracefully,
        sensuously,
in harmonious rhythm,
elegant branches
whispering beauty
to those who might see
the brief solo,
gone in a moment.

Travelogue

Voyagers no longer disembark
at decayed seaports,
    piers rotting
where sturdy ships once docked
      delivering the wealthy
          the hopeful,
    travel plans replaced
by accommodating airlines
getting us to destinations
        so quickly
there's no transition
between coming and going,
     just adaptation
       to climate change,
          time change,
when we conclude our journey.

Fundamentally

Death refuses
to go corporate,
historically dedicated
to individual enterprise,
only hiring temporary help
in times of plague,
    famine,
  holocaust,
mechanized war,
    any events
with massive fatalities
keeping the expenditure business
at full employment,
no fringe benefits
since non-unionized,
    no overtime
for the execution class,
just the endless task
disposing of the dead.

Enemies

We may have more enemies
then ancient Rome,
the most hated empire
   before the U.S.A.
Rome certainly had
   religious enemies
despite state tolerance
   of all religions.

The emperor and Senate
   never understood
    how one God,
    would not allow
    Jupiter and Mars
      to exist,
   though they weren't
      the one true God.

No other empire,
except for a few years,
expanded as fast
as The Persians,
    Rome,
   The United States,
And when those daring Greeks
   defeated Darius,
   defeated Xerxes,
they cleared the way
for Alexander of Macedon
   to rampage
across many lands
unexpecting his visitation
   until he arrived,
but didn't last long enough

for dynastic continuation.

But Rome, Rome,
the most sophisticated conqueror
that started with less
    than Athens,
but grew fast enough
to preserve and transmit
the cultural heritage,
    the foundation
of Western civilization.

And a piddling
    city state
fought and grew,
built roads, ships,
fought and grew
until the legions marched
across the known world,
only thwarted
by stubborn Germans
for hundreds of years,
recalcitrant tribes
refusing the benefits
of civilization,
resistance to be crushed
as long as the empire
had the means,
    the will
to crush opposition.

But Rome grew soft,
sated with riches
of a plundered world.
They still had the spirit
to fight the Goths,
but ignominious defeat
brought a new regime,

until Roman ways
seduced the wild Goths
and made them citizens
of an acceptant empire
that began to tremble
as the hoofbeats of the Huns,
      drew closer.

A miraculous victory
destroyed the Huns,
   saved Rome
from being sacked,
the last triumph
before descent to darkness.

Seasonal Awakening

The last snow has fallen.
After one furious blast
the cold wind has departed.
Crocus and forsythia
stir their sleepy roots,
cautiously dare to bloom.

Tired of shivering
we welcome warming days,
put away the scarf,
heavy sweater,
hope they won't be needed
until summer is long gone.

Accidents Will Happen

A man walks down the street
      ears covered
with hi-tech headphones
      playing music
from his IPOD,
carefully recorded
for his listening pleasure,
    and doesn't hear
    the warning sound
of a building falling on him.

A woman walks down the street
      eyes intent
on her smartphone's keyboard
    texting her friend
with urgent fingers,
describing her latest purchase,
    a new lipstick,
and she doesn't see
the oncoming bus
bearing down on her.

Ecce Homo

The beaten men
march downtrodden
through the ages,
forgotten faster
then generals or poets,
    brief fodder
of continuation,
obligations to species
    unrecognized,
      existence
a primal urge
spasmodically spermed
pleasure incidental
to continuation,
reproduction all,
from primal ooze
to footsteps on the moon,
haphazard evolution
shaping the ascent
of low brutes,
primitive, violent,
    producing
Beethoven, Mozart,
Auschwitz, Dachau,
mindless emissaries,
eruptions of despair
    compensated
by illogical hope,
    dedication
by the deviant,
the peculiar,
the creative,
to innovation,
implementation

extending racial survival
despite proliferation
of weapons of mass destruction,
    urgent for release
to perform the coda
of our final sonata.

Temperate Zone

A harsh winter
begrudges departing.
Our chilled flesh
craves warmth.
We look at cloudy skies
bringing more snow,
bundle up,
hat, gloves, scarf,
resisting the chill
that seeps into weary bones
worn down by sleet,
other assaults
on body heat,
awaiting better weather,
as long as climate change
does not remove Spring.

Separate, but…

The boss told me
I did a good job
and the extra hours
I put in last week
secured a big account.
He couldn't give me a raise
because the economy was poor:
'As soon as earnings pick up'…
But it didn't stop him
from a luxury vacation
in France and Italy.

Now is it just me,
or is that unfair?
I slaved for him
and got nothing.
He did little
and was rewarded.

I can't get a better job,
there aren't any,
so I should be grateful
for what I have,
but I can't help resenting
unequal treatment,
though I can't do anything
to change it.

Homeless

I served my country,
two years in Iraq,
four in Afghanistan.
Then I came home
to a foreign land
where I didn't fit in.
I had lots of problems
from years of fear and tension
expecting ambushes,
roadside bombs,
allies turning on us.
Yes I was disturbed.
They glibly call it
post traumatic stress disorder.
That doesn't make it better
to know it has a name.
I went to the V.A. Hospital.
They didn't seem to care.
They gave me an appointment
to see a doctor in nine months.
I told them my headaches
were getting worse,
but the indifferent nurse
wouldn't give me anything.
I can't go home.
My family doesn't want me.
I went to a shelter one night.
It was more dangerous
then sleeping on cardboard
on the sidewalk.
I don't know what I'll do.
Part of me just hopes
I won't flip out
and hurt someone.

Holiday

Explosions rip the night
but nobody pauses.
It's the 4th of July
and the fireworks show
erupts with color and sound
in a peaceful celebration
of a beautiful ideal,
a brilliant document,
a revolutionary concept
democracy,
though only for some.

Blue Jays

For years,
the Blue Jays came to our terrace,
competed with other birds
for seed.

Grown bolder
they came closer
and we fed them cashews.
It became clear
the way to a Jay's heart
was a succulent nut.

Despite my wife's admonitions
'they'd spit out peanuts',
we changed their diet
and they still came daily,
chased by pigeons,
harassed by doves,
menaced by robins,
and we enjoyed their beauty
without trying to tame them.

They brought their babies
who learned to eat nuts,
and grew up and had babies
who learned to eat nuts
and their antics gave us pleasure

Then one day they didn't come.
Nor a second, or third day.
After a week we missed them
and with all our worries,
personal, political, economic,
we had a new worry. What happened to our Jays?

Manhattan Landlord

I ran a swell restaurant
for many years
on a good block
in Manhattan.

I wasn't rich,
but made a good living,
paid my workers well
so they were happy
and passed it on to customers.

Then my lease ran out.
The landlord raised the rent,
three hundred percent.
There was no way
I could make money
paying that amount.

I tried to discuss my problem
with the landlord,
but he didn't care
if I went out of business.
He'd get more money
from the next tenant.

The economy was doing poorly,
except for the rich.
I told the landlord
if he raised the rent that much
I'd have to close my doors.
He didn't care.

Then I explained
I had twelve employees

who would lose their jobs,
and they had families
dependent on their income.
He didn't care.

I tried to negotiate,
said I would take home less
if my workers could keep their jobs.
I offered a one hundred percent raise
which would mean

I only broke even,
but my workers would be paid.
He didn't care.

I did everything I could
to make a deal
that would save the business
so all of us
could earn a living,
but his only response was:
'That's your problem'.
He just didn't care.

Limits

You promised
in front of a priest
to love, honor, cherish.
Then you started gambling,

When you lost
you started drinking.
The more you lost,
the more you drank.

You came home drunk,
yelled and cursed at me.
I had to help you to bed,
but you hit me.

Then you started beating me.
I begged you to stop,
but you said: 'It was my fault'.

I talked to my priest,
but he counseled patience.

The other night you hit me so hard
I had to go to the hospital.
You promised never again.

When I came home you cursed me
for not preparing dinner.
I have nowhere else to go,
but I can't go on this way.

If you hit me again,
I'll wait until you're asleep,
take a kitchen knife
and stab you in the heart.

Homeless II

I don't remember where I'm going.
I'm not even sure
if I had someplace to go.
Ever since my last stay at Bellevue
the meds they gave me
confused me even more.
I can tell
by all the people in the street
it's lunchtime.
I guess I'll go to Bryant Park
and see what I can scrounge
from the trashcans.
Those rich folk
always throw away
good food.

Holiday II

Detonations echo
across the city.
Security guards
are extra vigilant.
But the people are calm,
not worried about terror
as they briefly forget
ongoing concerns
in the annual display
on Independence day,
the fireworks show.

Blue Jays II

They've only been gone
 a week or so.
After all the years
coming to our terrace
I miss them already.

I do not know
why they're gone,
but the hazards of city life,
any life,
make survival difficult.

I remember how they talked
to my wife
and she talked back to them.

With all my concerns
crime, economic inequality,
the wars in the Mid East,
China, Russia, Iran,
I still worry about
the missing Jays.

 I cannot raise a posse
and search for them.
I don't know their names.
I can't even tell my Jays
from other Jays.

There's no point in hiring
a private detective.
The police would just laugh at me
if I declared them missing.
I may never find out. What happened to our Jays.

Digital Control

I sit at my desk,
another worker
in the Information Age,
and stare at my inbox
that conspires to prevent me
from returning to my screen,
by overwhelming me with paperwork.

Neighborhoods

You live in a city all your life,
go to playgrounds, school,
make friends, go on dates,
get a job, seek culture
in museums, theaters, the opera.
Then you go to a neighborhood
you haven't visited for years
and it's completely changed.
Hi-rises and up-scale shops
that used to be tenements,
Mom and Pop stores,
now departed,
as if never were,
as you will depart
unremembered
by the devouring city.

Homeless III

It rained for three days.
No one ate lunch
in Bryant Park,
so they didn't
throw away leftovers
in the trash cans.
I couldn't find a dry spot
to sleep at night
and my cardboard bed
got soaked,
so I threw it away.
Maybe if I'm lucky
I'll find a dry doorway
where no one will bother me,
but I've never been lucky.
If it rains for forty days
and forty nights
I'll probably drown,
but so will everyone else.

Holiday III

The explosions get louder.
My nerves are tingling.
Has war been declared?
I risk going closer
and hear 1930's music,
see people dancing happily
and I suddenly remember
it's the 4th of July.
Democracy may be fraying,
but we briefly escape
rampant inequality
in a brilliant display
of colorful fireworks.

Blue Jays III

For a brief moment
I thought I saw a Jay
sitting on the trellis
where they perched for years,
before coming closer for food.
Then a moment later
he was gone.
An illusion?
A ghost?
Wishful thinking?

I do not know
where they have gone.
I think of the pleasure they gave us
and hope they're still alive
and moved somewhere
to a nicer nest.

Matriculation

I graduated from college
in debt for student loans,
no friends to help me on my way,
no job opportunities.
My prospects were bleak.

I filled out job applications,
lied about where I worked,
various skills, experience,
to make me employable,
'but no one would hire me.

I lied to the landlord
about getting him the rent.
I lied to the utility company,
but they heard it all before
and shut off the power
leaving me in darkness.

I'm just about out of food
and help is not on the way.

I won't kill myself,
so my only choice
is to become a thief.

I'm healthy, fit and strong,
smart, well educated,
even personable.
I can learn quickly.

All I have to do
is decide what kind of crook
I want to be.

Diminishing Garments

The shorts get shorter,
        tighter.
The tops get smaller,
        snugger,
revealing more female flesh,
thighs, breasts, bellies,
then most girlie magazines
yet it doesn't seem to provoke
    public assault
in tolerant America,
and only Muslins are outraged
    by the wanton display
    of women's bodies.

Park Flow

The leaves of summer
begin to fall early,
fluttering to the ground.
When I don't look closely
I think butterflies.

Comparative Assessment

We look at the rich
    envious
of what they possess,
    all they enjoy
and we easily forget
while they're on their super yachts,
we have a comfortable apartment,
our children go to good schools,
we have enough to eat,
the occasional treat
a two week vacation
  somewhere nice.

Yet across most of the world
      poverty rules,
hunger, diseases, war,
ravages the people,
many of whom are happy
making do with little,
  but appreciating
whatever they have,
until disaster strikes
and there are few resources,
      or none
to ease infliction
and the daily suffering
restricts the search
  for daily bread.

Hunger, disease, violence,
    the separation
between joy and sorrow
accepted by millions,
neglected by millions,

so many self-absorbed
acquiring comforts,
    indifferent,
    too busy,
    too removed
from means of sharing
    abundance
with the needy world,
dreaming of the lottery,
    not realizing

    after taxes
there's barely enough
    to buy a Warhol.

So we trudge the worn path
    that our forbears trod,
many of us living better
    than anyone before,
        unfortunately
        never enough
to satisfy our primal greed.

Homeless IV

I stand forlornly
at the entrance to the park
rattling my paper cup
in the hope that passersby
will help me out
with some spare change.
I don't threaten anyone
and wait there patiently
expecting nothing,
most people in a hurry,
looking through me,
making me wonder
if I still exist.

Holiday IV

We celebrate the Fourth of July.
The French celebrate Bastille Day.
I forget what the Russians celebrate.
Potemkin Day? Karl Marx Day? May Day?
But does anyone remember
why we celebrate these holidays?
We all seem far removed
from revolutionary change
and except for the usual 1%,
we all want more material comforts
and most of us are unwilling
to cut off the heads
of the aristos,
substituting fireworks,
patriotic music,
for the Guillotine.

Blue Jays IV

After being gone for three weeks
the Blue Jay returned
to our terrace,
a bit shyly,
as if unsure of his welcome,
but he didn't fly off
when my wife put out peanuts.
He didn't stay long enough
for her to ask:
"Where have you been?"
He was a city Jay,
so he wouldn't take his family
on a trip to the country,
or the Hamptons.
He wouldn't ever
go to Coney Island.
Too Far. Too raucous even for a Jay.
A time share visit in Central Park?
No. Too many muggers.
I know he couldn't afford the Waldorf.
Maybe they just stayed home for three weeks,
hiding in the nest
like pretentious yuppies
who couldn't afford to go away
and hid at home,
so no one would know
they weren't out of town.
But he's back
and took a lot of nuts
before we went away
the next morning,
only for five days,
so his family
won't starve to death. Until we get back.

The Lessons of Empire

The Roman Senate
didn't have qualms
sending the legions
to conquer new lands,
crush rebellions
against their authority,
the only concern
domestic security.

The British empire
cruised the world
subduing unruly nations,
but cautious about
European competition,
yet never hesitated
to send the troops
to acquire new territory,
always with a moral pretext.

The American empire
started a little too late
to grab much more
then in its expanding neighborhood,
killing or robbing Indians,
Mexicans, French, Russians, Spanish,
and brought forth a great nation.

By the time we got to Europe
in World War I
the older dogs
had staked their claims
to Africa and Asia.
So after sour grapes
we chose self-righteousness
and became big brothers

to our underprivileged little brothers,
rather then land grabbers
and just ruled them
economically.

Weathervane

Winter is almost over,
    lashing out
with storm, snow, sleet,
reluctant to depart
and let us forget
that harsh climes
are here to stay.

From now on
brief summer
will hasten away,
    ushering in
    cold winds
to chill our bones.

Unequal Crisis

Construction in the city
goes on feverishly
for expensive condos,
new office buildings.
While on every avenue
restaurants are closing,
small shops shutting their doors,
because customers
can no longer afford
to shop, eat out.
The loss of jobs,
Mom and Pop stores
doesn't affect the rich
who can buy what they want,
as the poor struggle
as they always have
and the middle-class evaporates.

Homeless V

Lunchtime in Bryant Park
is the best time
to go through trash cans
and retrieve cans and bottles
for redemption, five cents each.
There's always leftover food
and liquid in the bottles,
so I manage to eat,
as long as it's nice out,
for when it rains,
people stay indoors
and I can't find anything.

Turmoil

Arms once raised in 'Heil',
now carry coffee cups
in a time of consumption
before resumption
of Information Age war
when tanks are a memory.

Now swift airstrikes
initiate missile attacks,
conserve the lives
of democratic troops
reluctant to be squandered
without meaningful purpose,
yet loyally obeying
incomprehensible orders
to fight limited battles
with confusing enemies
in Iraq, Afghanistan.

While the fading hegamon
still bestrides much of the globe,
the only sovereign power
willing to confront extremism,
as long as it doesn't offend
the peace loving people of Islam
who never seem to deplore
the brutal violence carried out
in the name of the prophet.

The decadent West,
whose wanton females
shamelessly bare their flesh
to the eyes of men,
tempting them to sin,

are the true enemy.

Admonitions
to reject calls to Jihad
are righteously ignored.
How else can evildoers
be redeemed for wrongful ways,
if they don't accept the true faith,
the only road to salvation?

Someone coined the phrase,
'Win the hearts and minds of the people',
a strategic fantasy of our leaders,
who never understood
the will of the enemy
is stronger than theirs,
who know without doubt
that sooner or later
we will abandon our allies,
leave our trucks behind,
withdraw our troops,
proclaiming victory.

This pronouncement
meant to disguise defeat
by a primitive foe
that had no jet fighters,
hi-tech missiles,
just an unconquerable will
that refused to crumble,
despite devastating assaults,
emerging victorious
over the oppressors.

While another great enterprise
by the bastion of democracy
failed ignominiously,

every setback a further erosion
of the spirit of America,
besieged on all sides
by friends and foes alike.

Possessed

Rapture
is not for everyone.
There has to be
a susceptible soul,
   self, persona,
some aspiring part of learning
      to accept possession,
           temporarily,
of delirious excesses
that allows elevation
without punishment,
or abrupt return to reality.

Vista

Disappointment,
frustration,
failure
a hard condition
affecting most of us
   who aspire,
      desire,
      security,
   a better life.

And if we have children,
   a hopeful future,
      easier
than the struggles of our parents
      for jobs, homes,
a livelihood in times of trouble
      that spare the rich,
      provoking envy
      in the needy,
who cannot understand
   an unfair system,
      yet accept
      inequality
as condition normal,
genetically imprinted
with the poverty gene
   inherited
through the ages
by almost all of us,
   consigned
to toil, military service,
   chores of society
that allow the wealthy
to dine at the tables of plenty,

while the rest of us
eat a meager crust,
yet cannot change
the final decision
    of harsh fate.

Caught

She caught me ogling her,
demanded:
'What the eff are you looking at?'
I felt like an idiot
fumbling for words.
'I thought I knew you,' I mumbled.
'You mean you thought you knew my tits!'
'No. Really.'
'You better get out of here,
before my boyfriend gets here.
He doesn't like guys staring at me.'
I slunk out, tail between my legs,
nervously wondering,
why I didn't have the nerve to say:
'I was looking at you, baby.'

Information Gap

We watch the news on tv
eager to learn
what goes on in the world,
and have no idea
how little we're told
about what really happens.
Most of us never notice
how stories suddenly disappear
and only reappear
if something occurs
that's too big to be concealed.
So what we find out
that may or may not affect us
is dependent on the owners
of the media,
mouthpieces for the wealthy,
servants, or fellow travelers.

Deceptive Words

The President addressed the nation,
explained why once again
we're going to war in a foreign land
that does not threaten us,
but is inexorably linked
to the war against terror.

I wonder if he understands
in a declining nation,
once the policeman of the world,
limited resources
are insufficient
to stem the barbarian hordes
clamoring for the blood
of civilized Westerners.

So our leader spoke loudly,
despite carrying a shrinking stick,
paid for with the taxes of the people
who continue to get poorer,
while the wealthy profit
from ongoing wars.

And leader after leader
gave us war after war
consuming our youth,
devouring our treasure,
while a resentful world
measured our decline,
waiting for the tide of history
to dwindle us to impotence,
so aggressive nations
can conquer other lands
we no longer protect

We squandered our resources
in consuming interventions
that left us destitute,
barely able to resist
envious competitors.

The tragic fall
of a great empire
was caused by overreach,
led by the greedy few
reaping obese profits
at the expense of the people,
who foolishly believed arrogant leaders.

Homeless VI

I know I smell.
I may be on the street,
but I'm not stupid.
Regular people have no idea
how hard it is to grab a shower.
The doc at the V.A.
told me to take my meds
and go to a shelter.
I couldn't sleep
when I took the meds.
When I went to the shelter
they beat and robbed me.
So I don't have a choice
and live on the street.
Sometimes I think about my rifle.
If I had it now
I'd visit the V.A.
and visit the shelter,
so all I can think about
is the way it used to be,
before I went to Iraq.

Emergency Aid

Conditions of life
change rapidly,
often too fast
for us to adapt,
so we suffer
flood, fire, war, disease.
The fortunate,
the sheltered,
survive
and accept the words
of reassuring leaders
that help is coming soon.

Fib, or …

It is easier to lie
then tell the truth.
Deception
comes naturally
to many of us.
Motives vary,
trying to spare sensitive feelings,
conceal a crime,
ego enhancement,
preserving one's job.
Most of us, now and then,
bend the facts a little,
but still express
righteous indignation
when called a liar.

Proportionate Response

Some of us believe
a fib, a little white lie
is not a sin.
And if it's done
in innocence
it's not a grievous fault,
especially when
it's meant to spare the feelings
of a sensitive loved one.

Yet others insist
the small lie
is the seed of deception
that grows into distortion,
propaganda, brain-washing.

So we use instructive adages,
'Honesty is the best policy',
'It's a sin to tell a lie',
to teach youngsters
the value of truth,
despite our living
in a dishonest world.

Unvalued Relics

The homeless sit in Bryant Park
shunned by passersby
who refuse to meet their eyes,
avoiding recognition
that might require admission
something is drastically wrong
when the outcasts of despair,
thoroughly dehumanized
by a heartless system
that has forgotten obligations
to the needy, the lost,
many of them veterans
who served their country,
shed their blood,
but can't adapt to their country,
become strangers in an alien land
where they no longer have a place,
where gunfire may be infrequent
compared to Iraq, Afghanistan, Vietnam,
and the streets not as dangerous,
except for the vulnerable.

With nowhere else to sit
in an unwelcoming city
the homeless drift to public parks
perhaps seeking a bit of nature,
a quieter environment
then noisy city streets,
maybe even restfulness,
mostly oblivious
to the day to day things
many of us take for granted,
no longer able to relate
to normal activity,

sleeping, working, recreation,
diversionary relics of the past
now only obscure memories,
incoherent glimpses
of what used to be.

Cityscape

Each street
a living, breathing
fragment of the fabric
holding together
aspirations,
desperation,
functional enactment
to the livelihood
of individuals,
the urban mass,
many struggling to survive
a harsh environment
unsympathetic
to hunter/gatherers.

Advanced Forecast

It is still summer,
yet cool winds begin to blow
hinting of a cold winter,
when the aging will sicken
    and die.
The poor will live in discomfort,
not able to afford fuel
heating demands unmet,
insufficient income
driving some to despair,
    some to crime,
others to resignation
hoping to endure
diverse tribulations.

Gunfire Serenade

Gunshots ring out again,
the home, school, church,
even the mall,
sacred shopping interrupted
by psychotic enactment
suddenly shattering lives,
abruptly terminated
in unexpected locales.

Homeless VII

One wheel is broken
on my shopping cart
and I can't fix it.
The guys at the supermarket
are real watchful these days,
so I can't swipe another one.
Maybe I can snag
one of those postal carts
with the cloth sides,
so no one can see
what's inside.

Park Entertainment

A Broadway show
comes to Bryant Park,
a musical, of course,
safer then serious drama,
or controversial comedy.
The actors sing, dance,
highly skilled,
but their voices lack
warmth, emotion,
the vital qualities
that make music move us.
Yet this is a free show
and I can't help wondering
why people pay
$125, or more, a seat
for impersonal entertainment.

National News

The media tell us
the economy is improving
and the well-to-do,
the comfortable
believe them.
Yet the poor
struggling to survive,
the middle-class
of diminishing income,
no longer accept
reassuring pronouncements
that things are improving.

Urban Reaches

Alone in a great city
strangers pass,
intent on jobs, crime,
shopping, terror.
I know not what.
They all look remote,
don't say 'good morning',
don't meet my gaze,
except the hostiles,
when I quickly look away.
I cannot tell
who is good, kind, normal,
smart enough to build a future.
Temporarily marooned
in a vast enclosure
I do not know what to do
to establish an identity.

Allotment

The sun is shining
on a beautiful summer day
and those who have jobs
go to work dutifully,
perhaps not happy with their fate,
but more cheerful then many,
whose homes were foreclosed,
whose lives won't improve
in the land of plenty,
where there's never enough
for everyone.

Righteous Speech

We removed Saddam Hussein
because he was an evil man
gassing his people,
developing nuclear weapons,
a threat to world peace.

So elected leaders
of the good old U.S.A.,
self-appointed
international policeman,
decided arbitrarily,
against some sensible advice
that state building
replacing tyranny
with democracy
is a difficult task
in an alien land
without due process,
or civil rights,
and a fanatic clergy
opposed to Western ways.

But our elected leaders
ignored warning signs
and decided.
Saddam must go.

So we invaded Iraq,
crushed feeble resistance,
a super power

flexing its military,
and we excavated Saddam
from his hiding hole
and swift justice followed.

So we helped install
a new government
that didn't know how to govern,
in a land divided
by race, religion, tribe.
And we proclaimed to the world
democracy was born.

But unrest was everywhere
and conflict spread
across the land.
And we withdrew our troops
and self-appointed bureaucrats,
as chaos prevailed.

Our elected leaders announced:
'Our mission is complete'.
A newly elected
democratic government
rules the land,
so we met our goals.
Our virtuous troops
brought freedom
to a long suffering people.

But when the government
couldn't govern,
and religious strife,

the lust for power,
erupted into bloody war
we looked the other way.
It wasn't our problem anymore.

Our elected leaders never asked
was Iraq better off with Saddam.
And we'll never know
if they lied to themselves,
lied to us,
or were just demented.
But the benefit of democracy,
is we get what we deserve.

Homeless VIII

They robbed my cans
for the second time
in a week.
I hustled my ass off
getting those cans
and got nothing for it.
At least they didn't beat me.
Maybe I'll get me a knife
and cut them good
if they try to rob me again.

Celestial Reckonings

A primitive space vehicle
after many years
finally reached Pluto,
the planet, not-a-planet,
and discovered water,
at least ice formations
that could be water.
At the current rate
of space travel progress,
if we survive
nuclear, chemical,
biological war,
climate change,
other disasters,
we might reach Pluto
in two or three hundred years,
barring a scientific breakthrough
just in time to find out
the water is polluted.

Camera Serenade

The tourists come
to Bryant Park,
take photos of statues
of they know not who,
photos of the carousel,
photos of the chess players,
the jugglers, ping-pong,
yoga on the lawn,
photos, photos, photos,
digital substitutes
for personal involvement
in all the events
crammed into a tiny park.

Fading Pleasure

Culture lovers
are a minority
without rights,
privileges,
just desire
for the arts.
Beethoven is alien
to most humans,
so is Picasso,
T.S. Eliot,
an endless list
of creators
appreciated by fewer
and fewer,
as the Information Age
encourages the spread
of the common denominator.

Pity the Children

The changing nature
of a liberal society
committed to tolerance
of the unreasonable,
the unacceptable
by any moral standards
that allow horrific crimes
inflicted on children,
while apathetic citizens
never rise up in outrage
and demand harsh punishment
for violent abusers.

Clamor

Prolonged discussions
of political or social issues,
controversial events,
rarely lead to agreement,
most ending in argument,
irreconcilable dispute,
intentions invariably
on self-assertion,
inflicting opinions
on unappreciative listeners.

Trauma Time

Virtue is no longer a virtue
in a land of tolerant intolerance.
The spoiled offspring of privilege
stroll through city streets
creatures so absorbed in entitlement
they cannot conceive that disaster
will ever target them,
armored in middle class comforts,
oblivious to others
until the sudden shock
of abrupt interruption
halts their serene conversations,
compels them momentarily
to confront harsh reality.

Conflict

Armies march in many lands.
Rebels attack in many lands.
Conflicts simmer across the globe,
      boil over,
        erupt
in deadly violence,
destroying lives,
   property,
   eradicating
aspirations for stability,
   disallowing
    normal pursuits,
      education,
   home building,
   raising children,
      hoping
tomorrow will be better
then the savagery today.

Rotations

We do not know why we are born
because we cannot question
until we have maturity
and relearn curiosity
to seek answers from elders.
And if we do not know wise men
we must search confusing books.

The need for understanding
does not affect everyone,
preoccupied with daily tasks
to provide food, shelter, clothing,
to their loved ones, dependents,
while those elected, appointed
to serve the people, the nation
do not always do their duty.

In the clash of interests
between the haves and have nots
rulers usually decide
in favor of the privileged,
whose wealth, resources, influence
allows retention of power
for cooperating leaders.

When we come into the world
without the means of advancement
we are creatures of coincidence,
nothing assuring accomplishments
except brains, talent, acquired skills,
opportunity discovered
by accident, luck, chance,
a haphazard path to the future.

Those dissatisfied with status quo,
demanding comprehension
of the forces that control us
are destined to be exiles
from the comforts of the system,
malcontents identified,
opponents to a sterile life.

Short Duration

Unless we are fortunate,
        inflictions
        visit regularly,
        affecting
the search for joy
often neglected
in the search for subsistence,
        easy for some
a tribulation for many,
        ingested
in a world of plenty,
    so divided,
    so chaotic,
that few prosper,
must do without,
while the comfortable
    never notice
the suffering of the multitudes.

Record Keeping

Across the world
  wars rage,
   so many
I did not know
there were so many ways,
so many reasons
to kill each other.

But we are consistent
in never allowing peace
  to last very long,
always ready to respond
to the call for battle,
death and destruction
  our heritage,
our recurring gift
to our children
to continue violence,
  more savage
then our forbears
who could not conceive
of the power we created
  to eradicate
   our enemies.

Abundant Tears

Confined on a tiny sphere
in a vast universe,
humanity seethes
with anger, hatred, greed,
driving the engine of war,
    terror,
      acquisition,
  acts of destruction
on a battered globe
  not large enough
    to shelter us
from violent assault
  on daily efforts
to endure encroachment.

Summer Parkscape

Summer brings tourists, shoppers,
workers, idlers to Bryant Park.
The various tourists,
domestic or foreign,
look pretty much alike
in the Information Age,
wardrobes by internet.
The workers wear
business clothes,
neat, formal, respectable,
intent on brief escapes
from office constriction.
Only idlers, mostly poorly dressed,
hang out purposelessly,
no urgent distraction
impelling them to motion.

Business as Usual

A corporation
markets its product,
car, medication, whatever,
and later we discover
it's defective,
and lose life, limb,
tranquility,
permanently disrupted
because in the lust for gain,
profit more important
than the public well-being.

Degrees

The big lie
to get a job,
to establish credit,
to get a girl,
to get a better grade in school,
is a deceptive tool
consciously designed
to acquire our desires.

The great lie
by kings, presidents, tyrants,
convinces the people
they will not go hungry,
they're fighting for freedom,
things will get better,
allows the leaders
to do as they will
and appear to be honorable.

Accused

'But I didn't do it, your Honor',
I told the judge,
despite the evidence against me,
joining the ranks of the accused
who always plead 'not guilty',
whether a traffic ticket,
murder, arson, rape,
reassuring the public
we are all innocent.

Lesser Choices

Some of us start lying
at a young age
for self-protection,
self-enhancement,
obtaining objectives,
diverse motives
inevitably arising
from conditional weakness.

Patterns of Deception

Fortune favors the fortunate,
the ambitious with ability
those born rich,
those willing to do
whatever has to be done
to get ahead
in an unjust world.
And those filled with desire
for material things
will lie, cheat, steal, kill
to get what they want,
while our teachers tell us
'honesty is the best policy'.

Common Practice

What should we think
when the President tells us
the economy is doing better,
while so many of us
are struggling to survive?
Should we be glad
the rich are doing well?
After all, they're human.
At least they used to be
before they joined a separate species,
those possessing plenty.
And as most of us decline,
victims of poverty,
we should be consoled
that some will survive
protected by prosperity,
while the rest of us
devolve.

The More Deceived

Yearning for the past
is the thermometer
of the present,
measuring dissatisfaction,
a common phenomenon
afflicting many,
who believed the promises
of elected leaders
that all will be well.

Urban Polluters

The traffic of the city,
human, vehicular, robotic,
goes from place to place
only impeded by congestion,
intent on destination,
unexpected delays
preventing timely arrival
mostly inconsequential,
except the urgent police car,
the urgent ambulance,
where a few minutes
makes the difference
between life and death.

Candidate

Politicians run for office,
fill the air
with pledges, promises,
lusting for privilege,
urgent to succeed,
presenting different faces
to different constituents.
As soon as elected
memory loss sets in,
the only priority
reelection,
far more important
than the public good.

Damming the Electronic Stream

Is Times Square still considered
the crossroads of the world?
In the Information Age
electrons are the travelers
and except for local restrictions
of forbidden transmissions,
the unstructured data flow
is barely comprehended
by social media users
consumed by the inane,
while the rich and powerful
establish control
of the data highways.

Welcome Mat

The ongoing search
for intelligent life
in the universe
should start at home,
in our dumbing down Earth,
where we're in desperate need
of solutions to our problems.
Obviously, the scientists
broadcasting our whereabouts
and our level of civilization
expect benevolent aliens
to make first contact.
What if it's Pizarro E.T.,
and his conquistadors
seeking treasury and glory,
or whatever they lust for
and it probably ain't Earth girls,
from the primitive nations
more concerned with killing each other
then resisting invasion from outer space.

Onslaught

We go about our daily
        routines,
those of us who have business,
jobs, shopping, social life,
all the activities
common to civilization,
only interrupted
by war, plague, disaster,
that thwarts plans
to build, create, acquire
whatever we desire,
while the fortunate
are allowed continuation
after the crisis is over.

Pressure Points

Most of my life
was a constant time
of urgent demand,
with exquisite highs
and agonizing lows.
Now that daily existence
is completely changed,
I must manufacture
a sense of urgency
to carry out
vital tasks.

Summer Pace

Weekend in the city
in the not as long
erratically hot summer,
courtesy of climate change.
The tourists, shoppers,
even the locals move slower,
whether torpid from heat,
not as urgent to acquire
goods, services, culture,
they just amble along
from place to place,
not looking happier
in a time of stress,
but not in a hurry,
an unaccustomed sight.

Medical Visit

Another doctor's appointment,
the same smug faces
complacent in their knowledge.
They don't care
about what they don't know.
Condescending to their patients
egos barely concealed
by assumed authority.
Yet they drink, use drugs,
have anxiety attacks,
all the inflictions
that others have,
only revealed
in suicide statistics.

Summertime

Everyone moves a bit slower
in the stifling heat,
crankier then usual,
more irritable.
Traffic is grumpier
despite most drivers
comforted with air conditioning,
yet tempers are on edge
and any disruptions
to smooth travel
can start an incident
leading to road rage.
That's the current term,
because it happens on the road,
but it starts somewhere else
and only erupts
when someone loses control.

Civilization

Civilization,
whatever that may be
in a society
that commits mass murder,
poisons the environment,
abuses its children,
nevertheless
presumes to be cultured,
creating music, art, theater,
for those who can afford it.
The rest do without,
unless they master the system,
or practice crime.

Stadiums

I found myself thinking
that wherever you go
in America
there are baseball fields,
a unique sports configuration
designed for folks to play ball.
I've never seen a baseball field
anywhere else in the world.
There are baseball fields in Japan,
Canada, Cuba,
but I've never seen them.
What does it say
about the national sport
when it's only been exported
to a few countrys?

Excuses

Some day,
a group of scholars
with nothing better to do
will make a dictionary,
a lexicon, an encyclopedia
of excuses.
The only issues to be debated,
will it be in alphabetical order,
listed by type, by dumbness,
originality?
They could write doctoral theses
about categories,
and each scholar would have an excuse
why his/her opinion is best.

Declarations

Our leaders promise
to fight terror.
We believe them.
Our leaders assure us
the economy is improving.
Some of us believe them.
Our leaders insist
they care about our problems.
A few of us believe them.
In a land of declining trust
after years of deception,
our leaders are still outraged
when we don't believe them.

Acknowledgements

Poems from Ignition Point have appeared in:
A New Ulster, Aberration Labyrinth, Antarctica Journal, Anti-Heroin Chic, Blue Collar Review (Partisan Press), Creative Writing Outloud, Fine Lines, Fragments of Chiaroscuro, Grey Sparrow Journal (Grey Sparrow Press), Light Journal, Literary Heist, Metaphor Magazine, Orbis Quarterly International Literary Journal, Page & Spine, Peeking Cat Literary Journal, Pegasus Magazine (Kentucky State Poetry Society), Plum Street Tavern, Polseguera, Published Poet, Pulsar Poetry, Rising Phoenix Review (Rising Phoenix Press), River Sandha Review, Scritura Literary Magazine, Sctu, Syndic Literary Journal, The Chicago Record, The Magnolia Review, The Miscreant, The Neglected Ratio, The Remembered Arts Journal, The Stray Branch, VerseWrights, Walking is Still Honest Press, Wilderness Literary Review (Wilderness House Press), Wildflower Muse, WINK: Writers in the Know

About the Author

Gary Beck spent most of his life as a theater director/playwright. He has an extensive collection of chapbooks, short story collections, novels, and poetry books. Gary's original plays and translations of Moliere, Aristophanes, and Sophocles have been produced Off-Broadway in New York City, where he resides.